How far was the London residential property market overvalued in the early 2000s?

Barry Vale

Contents

Abstract

Literature Review

Introduction

Chapter One – the Theoretical considerations in relation to the value of the London residential property market

Chapter Two - the Practical factors affecting the value of the London residential property market

Abstract

The following study has the objective of examining whether or not the London residential property market was actually overvalued or not in the early 2000s. To examine the issue effectively and as thoroughly as possible, all relevant theoretical frameworks as well as practical examples of the factors involved in the pricing levels are examined. As will be discussed there are various theoretical and practical influences upon the strength of the London residential property market. All relevant theoretical frameworks can help students of property management or business to understand trends, and could be used to predict pricing trends or changes of value within residential property markets such as the one in London. Most important will be cost-benefit analysis, risk management, and theories that relate to the supply and demand of products within markets. It was also considered whether the PEST business modal would be useful in predicting market values including overvaluations. PEST is a business modal that has been in use since the 1950s and undoubtedly retains relevance in the form of the updated PESTEL version.

Trends, developments, and also alterations within the practical factors that contribute to the pricing levels of the London residential property market will also need to be evaluated and fully understood. The discussion will also examine the features that are either unique or at the very least, more pronounced in the London residential property market in comparison with the domestic housing market in Britain as a whole.

Some of the factors that are considered as well as being

analysed below could be argued to be economic and also political factors that have an impact upon the London residential property market just as issues more overtly viewed as being exclusive to property management or business studies. Economic, political, social, and demographic influences upon the overvaluing of the London residential property market will be mentioned to present a better balanced and more accurate analysis of that specific market.

Also included is a Literature Review that describes the usefulness and the areas of information in which the books and other references used to write the dissertation were put to.

Literature Review

The Penguin Dictionary of Economics by Bannock, Baxter, and Davis was used as a general reference in relation to the economic theories put forward in this dissertation. It was useful for the ideas relating to supply and demand, besides the potential impact of altering interest rate levels. Understanding the affect of supply and demand as well as the factors that change it are fundamental to predicting and evaluating fluctuations in market values. The book was also useful for theoretical concepts that are relevant for determining and predicting market values, cost-benefit analysis, as well as risk management.

The Daily Telegraph article - London property market: London eye, Prime properties are still selling fast, but super-rich buyers are watching carefully to see how the financial markets recover by Lulu Egerton was used to gain information about the apparent strength of the more luxurious properties within the London. This article was used to evaluate whether the location and the size of different residential properties has an impact upon which segments of the London market are most likely to be overvalued, and if those segments are easier or harder to have their value accurately predicted. The material within this article tends to support the contention that houses within the most popular and therefore the most expensive districts of London are less likely to be affected by economic recessions than residential properties in the least expensive districts of the city. It helps to uphold claims that values within specific markets could be predicted with varying degrees of accuracy as well as providing astute evaluations of contemporary market values.

Central Debates in British Politics by Fisher, Denver, and Benyon was used for reference in relation to the less desirable consequences that the sell off of council houses has had upon the London residential property market. This book was used to support the argument that the right to buy scheme still has a profound influence upon the valuation of residential property in London, as it means that the availability of affordable housing has been reduced over the long-term. The logical assumption is that scarcity leads to residential property becoming overvalued, scarcity that central government housing policies can increase or decrease. This book was also useful for other changes in economic policies that could impact upon the market being examined.

UK Residential Property Review - Report from Grant Stanley, Chartered Surveyors for January 2006 was used as a source of information with regard to ongoing valuation trends within the London residential property market. This review mentions the strengths and the weaknesses within the domestic housing market in London, and includes reasons for variations in value and prices within that market. The article also mentions reasons for the residential property market in London being stronger than within the rest of the country.

Investigating Town Planning by Greed provided information about both immediate post-war housing policies as well as the policies of the Thatcher and Major governments and their impact on the London residential property market. The main reason for referring to this book was to demonstrate the practical impact that the policy decisions of the central government can have upon the supply of residential property within the London area. The reason for evaluating actual and potential central government involvement in the supply of residential property is that it can be useful for predicting the availability of affordable and unaffordable housing stock.

The complete guide to investing in property by Hodgkinson was used as reference for the ways in which investment decisions are made as well as theoretical concepts relating to the valuation of residential properties. Hodgkinson contends that the key for successful investment in property is to understand the risks involved when buying property and subsequently reselling it or renting it out to maximise profits. The book focuses on the methods by which individuals, businesses, and organisations could gain the most benefits from the property markets. Hodgkinson also argues that good sales technique, the style of houses, as well as the locations of properties all play a part in determining market values. PEST is useful in allowing investors, buyers, and sellers to predict the direction in which property values are going in, yet sound judgement or good luck can make all the difference between success and failure.

From Beveridge to Blair – The first fifty years of Britain's Welfare State 1948-98 by Jones and Lowe was used to help explain why the central government intervened in the London residential property market after the Second World War. Again this book was used in relation to the impact of the right to buy scheme and other economic policies pursued by the Thatcher government had upon the London residential property market. It was also useful with reference to why New Labour did not drastically alter housing policy after 1997.

The Draft Mayor's Housing Strategy - Consulting on London's housing by the Mayor of London office was used to examine how proposals the level of affordable could potentially have an impact upon the London residential property market. The Mayor's Housing Strategy could certainly have practical affect upon market values as it proposes to increase the supply of affordable housing. This document demonstrates that there is now more political intention to intervene in the London residential property market to lower the housing costs, which are making it harder for people to afford adequate accommodation. In terms of PEST as well as supply and demand theories the construction of greater quantities of affordable housing should lead to a reduction in the overvaluation of existing properties.

Politic and Governance in the UK, by Moran was used to provide information and give depth to the section about the impact that the right to buy scheme has had upon the value of housing within the London residential property market. That information was used to back up the assertion that the right to buy scheme has increased the long-term tendencies of residential properties in London to generally rise in value well above the national average for Britain

Urban and Environmental Planning in the UK by Rydin was also used to gain information about the tendency of the London residential property market to become overvalued, especially after the right to buy scheme had an impact on the supply of residential properties within that market.

Building Economics by Seeley was used as reference for the theoretical and the practical issues with relation to the economics of the construction and property development industries. The point of this information was to argue that residential property values are higher in London as land, labour, and construction materials cost more in the London area, though it produces higher levels of wealth for some people than the rest of Britain.

The City – In Time and Space by Southall was used for information that related to the impact that the construction of new towns had upon the London residential property market in the immediate post-war period. The point that this information was used for was to argue that demographic changes whether planned or inadvertent are capable of profoundly affecting the value of residential property in London. Basically if the population increases then the need for housing also increases, whilst if the population falls or is moved somewhere else then the need declines. Demographic changes especially if unexpected can make housing markets change with little chance of being accurately predicted.

The Independent article- London residential property is the most expensive in the world by Jane Padgham, from the 08 May

2007 was used as a source of information about the high prices and rent levels currently being experienced in the London residential property market. This article was useful for explaining the reasons for some parts of the London residential property market remains overvalued despite unfavourable economic conditions and the prospect of more affordable housing being built in the next few years.

The Sunday Times article of June 10, 2007 - The London property market by Peter Conradi was used as it mentioned the current growth rate in prices in the London residential property market.

Knowing the present growth rate of prices and valuations are helpful in making predictions of future market trends. When prices and values have enjoyed long periods of expansion then investors and financial institutions will take greater risks on continued growth and will accept unrealistically high valuations.

Further information about the PEST business modal was also obtained from the website www.ProvenModels.com to assist in the arguments that are put forward below.

Introduction

This dissertation will discuss the arguments in favour as well as arguments against the notion that the London residential property market is overvalued or correctly valued. Residential property markets can often gain reputations for being undervalued or overvalued, perceptions that may or may not be borne out by reality or an analysis of actual pricing levels within each residential property market. The under valuation, and sometimes alternatively the overvaluation of residential property markets could last over a long-term period, or conversely such trends could happen for a short-term period. Some locations may be more or less likely to enjoy long-term periods of high property prices, and will sometimes be regarded as having overvalued price levels within their respective residential property markets. The London residential property market has often been cited as an example of a residential property market that experiences such trends that are conducive towards higher property prices, and possibly overvalued values. A mixture of property management strategies, marketing ploys, geographical locations, and last but no means least economic trends are all factors that have a strong influence over the value of the London residential property market. These trends or factors could lead to the overvaluation of residential properties or less likely the under valuation of such properties (Bannock, Baxter, & Davis, 2003 p.91).

There are various organisations, which make decisions and provide housing to rent or to buy that potentially contribute to the overvaluation or the generally high prices witnessed within the London residential property market (Bannock, Baxter, &

Davis, 2003 p.91). Such organisations include local authorities, the central government, property rental companies, estates agents besides Registered Social Landlords. Private individuals have also contributed to high housing prices, as they have sought to either invest in residential property or to gain a roof over their heads (Hodgkinson, 2007 p. 70). Housing in London is therefore provided by both private and public sector organisations, with houses to buy or to let. Private banks, finance companies, building societies, and also the Bank of England have a vital impact upon the health and strength of the London residential property market. The importance of banks in general, and the Bank of England in particular is related to the amount of money that people are able to borrow, as that often separates those that can acquire mortgages to buy their own property from that have to rent. Since the Bank of England was given control of setting interest rates it has published details of its monthly meetings, a valuable source of information for any organisation using PEST to predict market trends, and a cause for concern for people with mortgages (Bannock, Baxter, & Davis, 2003 p. 20). For those people that are unable to obtain mortgages or that are not prepared to find high repayment levels are faced with the option of renting residential properties within the London area instead. The high residential property prices in the London area is regarded as an attractive reason for renting housing as buying property is out of the financial reach of increasing numbers of people aiming to move into, or to remain within the area. Variations in the cost of borrowing will it shall be argued alter the balance of the London residential property market, perhaps changing the degree of overvaluations and affecting pricing levels too (Hodgkinson, 2007 p. 70).

The cost of borrowing as will be examined in greater depth in the subsequent chapter is many would contend actually pivotal with regard to the rental and the residential property purchase price levels which are charged in the confines of the London residential property market. The cost of borrowing, besides the over all amounts of indebtedness will be analysed to note as well as to comprehend the affect all these factors have upon the overvaluation or otherwise of the residential property market within the London area. There is a general perception that there is a greater demand for residential and commercial properties in London for several reasons that when they are combined go a long way in explaining the higher property prices and also rent levels inside the immediate London area (Hodgkinson, 2007 p. 70). Varying degrees or levels of demand, residential property sales, and altering rental levels in the London residential property market are often recorded by different organisations, and thus could be used to predict future demands in the market besides recording past and present performance. The over all level of demand may be regarded as determining the profitability of residential property developers and real estate retailers whilst having a strong influence upon the affordability of housing for the people that actually need it to live in London. As will be discussed, demonstrated, and evaluated many property developers, private investors, estate agents, and banks have often enjoyed long periods of growth in the sales as well as the revenue generated by the London residential property market (UK Residential Property Review, January 2006).

The London residential property market has traditionally been recognised as being one of the highest priced residential housing markets in the world. Generally it has been housing costs and also residential rental price levels that have tended to be higher as many people have wanted to live and work in London. The geographical location of London alongside its position as the capital city of the United Kingdom has tended to increase the desire of people to live within the Greater London area. Property developers, Estate Agents and banks would not want to prevent people finding somewhere to live in the London area, as that would harm their capacity to make profits from their own involvement in the London residential property market. For such organisations it is beneficial for them to provide housing or the finances for people to buy houses which when coupled with high demand are frequently highly profitable. The concern for the organisations that make the greatest profits from the London residential property market being expensive is that the boom in related sales and rental revenues could end abruptly, for instance if there is an economic recession, or a substantial loss in market confidence (Hodgkinson, 2007 p.118).

Other organisations, most notably the central government and to a similar extent local authorities are also concerned about the value as well as the strength of the London residential property market. The central government has the power, if not always the desire to take steps that could alter the strength and performance of the London residential property market (Hodgkinson, 2007 p. 70). Central government has the ability to change the availability of housing not only in the London area but also across the whole of Britain. It will argued in the following chapter that one of the main factors determining the value of the London residential property markets is the scarcity of residential property in relation to the demands of people that want to be housed within the London area. Local authorities have in the past being tasked with providing affordable housing inside their respective district boundaries. The role of local authorities in this respect has been diminished as a consequence of the right to buy scheme with Registered Social Landlords taking a more prominent role. Also the much higher number of immigrants moving into the London area has had profound implications for the residential property market. The role of local authorities and Registered Social Landlords in the London residential property market is much less than that of private landlords, estate agencies, and property developers (Seeley, 1996 p.421).

The central government has to balance the effects of a highly priced London residential property market against the potentially harmful consequences of a crash in that market caused by economic recession or a loss in confidence. The central government used to have a greater influence over the strength of the London residential property market when it had the power to change the interest rate levels of the Bank of

England. The Bank of England now has complete control of its own interest rate levels and has shown itself prepared to increase those levels to maintain low inflation rates within the British economy. There is generally assumed to be a strong link between the Bank of England interest rate levels and the performance of the residential property market throughout the whole of Britain. There are however sound theoretical and practical reasons for examining the London residential property market separately (Bannock, Baxter, & Davis, 2003 p.91).

There are grounds for believing that using cost-benefit analysis, risk management techniques, and specific tools such as PEST could allow individuals as well as organisations to evaluate and to predict values within a specific market (Bannock, Baxter, & Davis, 2003 p. 77). These theoretical frameworks can if used properly by individuals, businesses, and organisations allow them to make the most of high prices and overvalued market conditions. However, if buying or selling residential property in favourable and unfavourable conditions is successfully predicted it does not guarantee success or failure for everybody. Shrewd or bad decisions by each individual, business, and organisation can bring success or failure that fits in with general market conditions or bucks the over all trend (Hodgkinson, 2007 p. 70).

PEST seems to be a highly suitable analysis tool with regard to ascertaining whether the London residential property market is overvalued. PEST actually stands for Political, Economic, Social, and Technological. The starting point for this modal is that businesses need to take all these factors into account when making decisions about improving their financial performance. Businesses need to understand the environments that they operate within; it will enhance their abilities to make sound decisions in terms of investment and expansion. PESTEL is an updated version of this modal that takes environment and legislation into account as well (www.ProvenModels.com).

Chapter One – the Theoretical considerations in relation to the value of the London residential property market

This chapter will examine the theoretical considerations and frameworks in relation to the issue of whether the London residential property market is currently overvalued or not. The starting point of all these theoretical considerations is the economic notion of demand, how that notion could be fully understood, how it could be accurately predicted, and the factors that are able to increase, decrease, or maintain the levels of demand. The full and accurate understanding, the predicting, and even the attempts to control demand is a highly important motivation for anybody that wishes to study markets. It would be useful as well as for the individuals and organisations that ideally want to gain the most from being actively involved in markets (Bannock, Baxter, & Davis, 2003 p.91). Whether the actual or the perceived consequences of demand are considered to be good or bad can depend entirely upon the nature of the market that is been studied or examined, not to mention the views of the people evaluating those markets in operation (Seeley, 1996 p.421). Without meaningful or substantial amounts of demand markets would not have developed in the first place, and would certainly not be maintained for long if all the demand vanished over night (Bannock, Baxter, & Davis, 2003 p. 91).

Too little demand can be even more damaging to market performance and sustainability than too much demand. Economists have known and discussed the importance of demand in both theoretical and practical terms for a long time. The linked concept of value is hardly relevant at all if there is no discernible level of demand for any particular goods or products that are provided via any specific market or economic sector (Hodgkinson, 2007 p. 70). Low or non-existent demand for goods and services logically entails that prices for those items alongside their relative value will thus always be low. Demand for some goods and services will always be stronger than for others, though astute marketing and advertising allows businesses opportunities to increase demand for their particular products. There should therefore for instance always be a higher consumer demand for human essentials such as food, drink, the utility services, and of most relevance for the London residential property market, the need for housing. Arguably the need for housing or adequate shelter is an essential human requirement, whilst property locations, housing standards, and over all comfort can vary greatly (Bannock, Baxter, & Davis, 2003 p. 91).

Demand in some respects can be managed or at least taken advantage of by private businesses and, other organisations that largely operate for profit. Private businesses and organisations will frequently use marketing campaigns as well as advertising to create extra demand for their goods and services to increase their profits. Businesses have to market their products to convince people to buy from them (Bannock, Baxter, & Davis, 2003 p. 91). Expanding levels of demand leads to the over all expansion of markets whilst also increasing the opportunities for businesses and organisations to make higher profits. Private businesses will be attracted to operate within the markets that promise to provide the greatest level of returns for the time and money invested in new projects, and the selling of new or existing products. Strong levels of demand in a specific market will attract both buyers and sellers into getting involved in investments or purchases. Property developers, estate agents, and also private landlords will have strong incentives to serve besides creating demand for customers to purchase property outright or to let (Hodgkinson, 2007 p.118).

Property developers, estate agents and similar organisations find it in their best interests to convince people to buy or to let the residential properties that they own or are selling on somebody else's behalf. Economic theorists contend that high levels of demand should increase levels of competition within specific markets, and also increase the level of profits that should be made (Hodgkinson, 2007 p.118). High levels of demand will also lead to a shortage of supply over the long-term, whilst increasing inflationary pressures within the British economy taken as a whole. The property developers, estate agents, private homeowners, and also landlords are generally happier to experience higher levels of demand as it improves their prospects of increasing the amount of money they make from the London residential property market. Banks and building societies are able to play their part in fuelling demand in the London residential property market by giving people the mortgages they need to buy residential properties within the London area, as well as upon a national basis. Strong levels of demand when coupled with increasing residential properties prices stimulates banks and building societies into lending ever greater amounts of money, though that raises the risks of people defaulting upon their mortgage or loan repayments. High interest rates and economic recessions increase the level of reprocessions and debt levels which can harm the profits of banks such as Northern Rock (UK Residential Property Review, January 2006). Using PEST should allow such organisations the ability to understand the relationship between political and economic factors; in order to make the best informed decisions to take advantage of demand levels and reduce losses during recessions (www.ProvenModels.com).

The central government theoretically has the power to affect the levels of demand within the confines of the London residential property market (Fisher, Denver, & Benyon, 2003 p. 14). The central government can encourage or attempt to discourage property developers and estate agents from the constructing of new housing projects inside the area that is covered by the London residential property market (Moran, 2005 p. 28). Besides encouraging new housing construction projects, the central government also has the power to tempt or persuade property developers and private investors to refurbish and also to modernise existing housing stock in the run down parts that are contained within the London residential property market area. Redevelopment projects have tended to concentrate on building business and also retail premises yet have sometimes prompted the new construction or renovation of residential properties (Hodgkinson, 2007 p.118). When redevelopment projects have revived businesses in previously run down districts then workers have often resorted to find nearby residential properties to live in (Daily Telegraph, 06/10/2007).

The central government directs national economic policy in the United Kingdom, which has implications for the levels of demand experienced within the context of the London residential property market. Basically during periods of strong economic growth and sound performance the demand for more residential housing increases whilst house sale prices and rental rates will also increase (Hodgkinson, 2007 p.118). Central governments prefer to preside over periods of economic boom rather than get the blame for recessions that would harm the London residential property market as well as increasing unemployment. Recession and economic down turns cause the contracting of overvalued markets, including property-related areas such as the London residential property market. Central governments have the option of building extra public sector housing, a change in policy that would alter the demand for private residential properties to buy as well as to let (Bannock, Baxter, & Davis, 2003 p. 396). Neither the Conservatives nor New Labour would return to the time when the public sector, that in the form of local authority controlled council housing owned a large percentage of residential properties. Although demand theories have been around for a long time, sometimes alterations in the markets are hard to successfully predict and are not adequately covered by theoretical notions that could be linked with the developments inside the scope of the London residential property market (Bannock, Baxter, & Davis, 2003 p. 91). Central government policy and legislation as much as the actions of private sector businesses could alter demand with little or no warning what so ever. For instance, one area in which the central government has had an inadvertent not to mention largely unpredicted influence upon the level of demand for housing inside the London residential property market, and that has been immigration policy. Unexpectedly high numbers of asylum seekers as well as workers from other European Union member states have come to the United Kingdom under New Labour since 1997. These particular migrants have mainly been concentrated in the London area and also in the South – East region of England (UK Residential Property Review, January 2006).

Supply is another theoretical concept that could be regarded as having an impact upon the overvaluation of the London residential property market. In market conditions that have an exact balance between demand and supply it would generally be assumed that all goods and services are bought as well as sold at their true market value (Daily Telegraph, 06/10/2007). On the occasions when there is not an exact balance between supply and demand, which means that value not to mention the price of goods or services will fluctuate as much as the levels of supply and demand change. Differences between supply and demand can lead to either deflation or inflation in the prices and values of all goods or services (Bannock, Baxter, & Davis, 2003 p. 91).

Abundant supplies or very low levels of demand will usually result in low prices and also low or limited value. High levels of supply tend to favour consumers and buyers as prices are kept lower and there is a wider choice of sellers to buy goods from.

Sellers on the other hand prefer it when demand outstrips supply leading to higher prices, as well as increasing the value of whatever they are actually selling (Bannock, Baxter, & Davis, 2003 p. 396). Demand can outstrip supply when sellers underestimate the number of consumers that want or need to purchase the items they are selling. Sellers tend to make or supply the number of units that they have sold before, as it is considered to be more cost effective that way. Businesses that are able to increase or decrease the supply of goods they sell should be in a position to maximise the value of such goods, as well as making the highest amount of profits available to them (Hodgkinson, 2007 p.118). Businesses have to work upon the assumption that supplies are finite to maximise their revenues and to minimise disruption for their customers. Organisations and businesses may not be responsible for the demand for products outstripping the available supply of such items, yet it should lead to greater levels of profit. On the occasions in which demand heavily outstrips supply the possibilities of markets as a whole and the London residential property market in particular becoming overvalued are increased further (Hodgkinson, 2007 p.118).

Although the items that are on sale become more expensive the majority of consumers will have to pay the higher price levels to make the purchases that they wanted to make in the first place. When demand comfortably outstrips the available supplies over a sustained long-term period both buyers and sellers should be aware that prices might become unrealistically high resulting in overvalued markets. When confidence in the strength of the market becomes too high, people should be aware of the consequences of that confidence collapsing. During periods of boom operating as a business within an overvalued market means that high profits are there for the taking yet the risks of a downturn in that market should never be discounted (Bannock, Baxter, & Davis, 2003 p. 91). Businesses and organisations have the choice of being cautious during economic booms or they could expand without thought of the consequences when recession makes prices and values plummet. Such an economic downturn occurred during 2004 and 2005 after the Bank of England raised interest rates leading to a decline in the sale of residential property as well as fewer mortgages being taken out. Banks and building societies have attempted to avoid reduced profits by offering remortgages, long-term fixed rate mortgages, and mortgage protection. Offering attractive remortgages packages allow banks to continue making money even when property markets are depressed (UK Residential Property Review, January 2006).

The theoretical notion of value is also fundamental for examining the contention that the London residential property market is overvalued or is realistically valued (Bannock, Baxter, & Davis, 2003 p. 396). Before goods, products, and services are sold within markets, the businesses or organisations selling them should calculate how much it costs to construct, make, and provide the items that they sell. To obtain a realistic idea of the value of any goods or services it is necessary to account for all the costs involved in making items ready for sale to the general public and also ensuring that maximum profits will be made (Hodgkinson, 2007 p.118). Some factors, which affect values within a market, are straightforward to evaluate and cost such as the cost of land or legal fees. Other factors that affect the value of residential property are more abstract, for instance the way in which a house is decorated can determine who will buy it and for how much (Hodgkinson, 2007 p.70).

When it comes down to working out the value of residential property the cost of construction, materials, land, and the facilities available in new housing need to be considered. Property developers and estate agents are in the best position to ensure that all new housing is sold or let out to customers with prices that reflect the full value of the construction costs. However, working out the value of residential property is not only based on construction costs, the location of the buildings and the style of the housing also determines value (Bannock, Baxter, & Davis, 2003 p. 396). Residential property in more fashionable districts of London will be more expensive to buy or to let than similar housing in less fashionable districts. People have a tendency to prefer to reside in quieter and less crime prone districts, meaning values rise quickly when other people have to find housing in other nearby districts (Hodgkinson, 2007 p.70). In that way periods of high prices will raise the value of residential property throughout given areas such as the London residential property market. Periods of high demand in the London residential property market should always lead to the housing in that area increasing its value. Given the scarcity of residential property in the London area there could be no surprises that prices are arguably overvalued within this specific market. The City of London finances the higher prices experienced in the most sought after postcode districts of London, alterations in the stock market could prove more damaging than increases in interest rate levels (Daily Telegraph, 06/10/2007).

Using the PEST business modal would allow organisations to effectively evaluate all of the theoretical considerations above to predict market trends as well as deciding if such markets are realistically valued. Most of the factors mentioned above are political, economic, and social in origin. Technological factors also have an important contribution to modern markets. Advances in information technology mean that businesses can obtain information sooner rather than later, and also have the opportunity to analyse trends earlier. The use of computers speeds up the time taken to carry out complex transactions within residential property markets yet misjudging political, economic, and social factors could lead to errors in the valuation of properties (www.ProvenModels.com).

Chapter Two - the Practical factors affecting the value of the London residential property market.

This chapter will evaluate the practical factors, which have arguably affected the value of the London residential property market. Some of these factors only had an impact upon the value of the London residential property market for a limited time, whilst other factors essentially have a continuously ongoing influence on the value of housing in the London area. Many of the practical factors that affect the value of the London residential property market are linked to the theoretical considerations mentioned in the previous chapter, factors that need to be considered through PEST business modals. Cost-benefit analysis, supply and demand theories besides PEST are only of use if they allow accurate evaluations and predictions of market trends (Bannock, Baxter, Davis, 2003 p. 77). When combined together practical factors and theoretical considerations allow a thorough evaluation of all things that affect the value of the London residential property market. The practical factors demonstrates the ways in which the London residential property market tends towards high housing prices and the assumption that by and large the residential properties within are overvalued (Southall, 2000 p. 338).

Demand for housing also acts as a practical factor as well as being a theoretical consideration that markedly affects the value of the London residential property market. The London residential property market has a long running tradition of having a higher demand for housing that the remainder of the United Kingdom, demand that has often spread to surrounding areas in the South East of England (Jones & Lowe, 2002 p.187).

Higher levels of demand have logically led to higher prices and valuations for housing within the London residential property market. The migration of people to London was an important factor that contributed to an accelerated growth rate that helped the city become one of the largest and also one of the wealthiest cities in the world (Hodgkinson, 2007 p.118). Indeed for long periods of time the level of demand for housing in the London area has outstripped supply, which in the past led the poorest people having to live in cheaper slum dwellings. They had to do so due to being unable to afford higher rent levels or not being able to buy their own residential properties. In recent years potential first buyers have decided to delay buying residential property as they find renting less of a financial burden than expensive mortgages and heavy debt burdens (UK Residential Property Review, January 2006).

In the immediate post-war period demand certainly outstripped the supply of residential property within the London area primarily as a consequence of housing destroyed during the Second World War. The post-war central governments came up with different strategies to meet the demand for residential property that reduced the housing shortages and restricted the overvaluation in the London area until the 1980s (Jones & Lowe, 2002 p.4). The first strategy for reducing the demand for residential property in the London area was the construction of housing estates in new town developments. The new towns were designed to reduce housing shortages in other cities such as Birmingham, and Manchester, yet London had more new towns than any other city in the country. The new towns built for London included Croydon, and Milton Keynes. Although new towns did reduce demand for residential property in London for a short period the continued expansion of the city has meant that the experience of higher house prices as well as higher rent levels never disappeared from the London residential property market (Southall, 2000 p.337). Another consequence of the new town was that it increased demand for new residential property in those respective areas, though green belt regulations restricted new housing construction, meaning that new houses had to be built in existing urban areas. Other factors have meant that the high prices within the London residential property market are currently higher than ever and increasingly prone to overvaluation (UK Residential Property Review, January 2006).

Another policy of central government during the immediate post-war period that was intended to meet the demand for housing was the expansion of council housing. Council housing schemes had originally began during the 1920s, yet a shortage of public funds had restricted the numbers actually built. The

Atlee government had seen the construction of millions of council houses as being vital for post-war reconstruction, which increased the availability of affordable housing (Greed, 1996 p. 77). The construction of council houses lowered the costs of letting throughout the London residential property market as local authorities charged lower rents than private landlords did. Although the price of buying residential property in the London area was higher than the national average the tendency for housing to become overpriced was reduced by the restrictions that people faced when they applied for mortgages (Southall, 2000 p. 337). As the banks and building societies were more averse to lending high amounts of money than they would be now (Greed, 1996 p. 77).

A greater number of residential property were made available by the building of prefabricated houses, high rise tower blocks and the renovation of unused houses. Such strategies prevented the London property market becoming overvalued despite rising property and rental prices during periods of economic boom (Rydin, 2003 p. 49). Not only did the demand for residential property seem to be met; sub-standard slum housing had become a thing of the past. The demand for residential property within the London area was increased by immigration into the United Kingdom in the 1950s and the 1960s. New Commonwealth immigrants generally moved into the inner city districts of London, as well as other cities such as Birmingham, and Leicester. The arrival of these immigrants made up for the number of people that left the London area to move into the new towns. Immigration could have had a greater impact upon the demand for housing within the London residential property market but for restrictions on the number of New Commonwealth immigrants from the early 1960s (Fisher,

Denver, & Benyon, 2003 p.12).

The tendencies for the London residential property market to become overvalued became more apparent in the early 1970s. The Heath government had come to office determined to lower inflation and resorted to increasing interest rates to counter the rapidly rising residential property prices in London and the South East of England. Heath reversed those economic policies once unemployment began to rise. The central government however was finding it difficult to fund the construction of new council housing throughout Britain as a whole (Fisher, Denver, & Benyon, 2003 p.10). The reduction in the construction rates of new council housing had an impact within the London residential property market as central government and the local authorities in London found it harder to meet the demand for residential property. The severe financial difficulties experienced by the Callaghan government culminated in the decision to take an emergency loan from the International Monetary Fund. Those financial difficulties meant that the construction of new council housing came to a temporary halt. Had the Callaghan government been re-elected, the housing situation within the London residential property market might not have altered as dramatically as it actually did (Moran, 2005 p.28).

The Conservative government headed by Margaret Thatcher intended to alter the social, political and economic shape of Britain with policies that certainly affected the London residential property market. Margaret Thatcher was determined to break the post-war political consensus, which had greatly extended the provision of social security, as well as expanding the size and the scope of the public sector. The publicly owned council houses throughout the country as a whole were just one example of the expanded public sector, which needed to be reduced to revive the British economy (Moran, 2005 p.28). For the Thatcher government the obvious way to reduce the amount of council housing was to expand the already existent right to buy scheme for tenants to purchase residential property from their respective local authority. Previously the right to buy scheme did not have a noticeable impact upon the availability and supply of local authority controlled residential property, as tenants had to have rented such property for 15 years. Whilst local authorities could use all the sale revenues raised by the original right to buy scheme to fund more new housing construction (Greed, 1996 p. 77).

The Thatcher government reduced the period that tenants had to have rented houses from their local authority to three years, at once expanding the number of people able to participate within the right to buy scheme (Rydin, 2003 p. 49). The impact of the right to buy scheme upon the London residential property market was increased due to the Thatcher government not allowing local authorities to spend 80% of sale revenues on new council houses, as well as denying them any funding to build replacement housing stock. The construction of new local authority controlled residential property halted to barely detectable levels within a couple of years of the Thatcher government taking office. It meant that the poorer members of society had to find higher rents to pay to private landlords or face becoming homeless. For central government a less favourable consequence was that the amount of public money spent on housing benefit increased sharply (Fisher, Denver, & Benyon, 2003 p. 14).

The first consequence of the right to buy scheme was that the sale of so many local authorities controlled houses provided a significant boost to the London residential property market. With many thousands of local authority tenants taking advantage of the right to buy scheme deciding whether to buy their homes to live in or instead selling their newly acquired residential property on for instant profits. The former local authority tenants whose residential property where located within the most desirable districts of London such as Belgravia and Knightsbridge were the people most likely to sell their homes as soon as they bought them (Rydin, 2003 p. 49).

The right to buy scheme raised the demand for residential property within the London residential property market, yet the supply of such residential property was not infinite. Local authorities had a reduced scope for providing council housing for those people that could not afford to buy residential property, which meant people had to pay higher rents to private landlords (Fisher, Denver, & Benyon, 2003 p. 14). For those people that were unable to rent council housing before the right to buy scheme was extended, the expansion of the London residential property market meant either higher rent levels or arranging a mortgage to buy a high priced and increasingly overvalued house. The 1980s were generally a decade of boom for property developers, estate agents, banks, and building societies due to the rising prices in the London residential property market, which were increasing faster than elsewhere in Britain (Moran, 2005 p.28). The economic policies of the Thatcher government had bought about recession as well as high unemployment, yet the right to buy scheme and increased levels of borrowing helped to fuel a recovery of the British economy. Once the inflation rate had fallen sufficiently the Thatcher government cut interest rates which further fuelled the expanded prices within the London residential property market. The boom in the London residential property market alongside that in the British economy in general started to be dented at the end of the 1980s when interest rates started to rise again (Bannock, Baxter, & Davis, 2003 p. 323). As more people now had got mortgages to pay after becoming homeowners the rising of interest rates was increasing effective at reducing inflation, at the cost of greater numbers of people losing their houses for being unable to repay their mortgages (Rydin, 2003 p. 50). Interest rates and the level of unemployment thus become important factors for PEST analysis to include (www.ProvenModels.com).

The high level of mortgage debts within the London residential property market had risen as a result of the property boom during the 1980s. Banks and building societies had lent too much money for people that would not otherwise be able to afford overpriced residential property. The recession of the early 1990s reduced the demand for housing within the residential property market besides sharply reducing the value of all such property. Therefore, the early 1990s were a difficult period for the London residential property market with depressed property prices, negative equity, as well as a record number of properties being repossessed. The London residential property market was certainly not overvalued during that period with previously overvalued property quickly falling in price and value. Ironically the recession of the early 1990s did not affect the over all value or performance of the London residential property market as profoundly as some people had feared. High interest rates had made the recession of the early 1990s worse but the government of John Major maintained high levels to show its political commitment to the Exchange Rate Mechanism to the other members of the European Union (Bannock, Baxter, & Davis, 2003 p. 21). The humiliating British exit from the Exchange Rate Mechanism led to lower interest rates and inadvertently speeded up the process of economic recovery. Rising or at least recovering housing prices and performance within the London residential property market reflected economic recovery from the middle of the 1990s (Rydin, 2003 p50). Government economic policy therefore needs to be closely monitored for PEST analysis to predict altering values in the London residential property market (www.ProvenModels.com).

The recovery of prices and performance inside the London residential property market was greatly assisted by the continued shortage of the supply of residential property within the London area. In the absence of new housing construction by local authorities, the slow rate of construction of residential property by private property developers and also by Registered Social Landlords has failed to meet supply. Insufficient supply of residential property within the London market soon led to property prices and rental levels rising again as well as the tendency for the market to become overvalued. Unlike the Thatcher government, the government of John Major was concerned about the inadequate supply of new buildings within the London area. The efforts of the Major government to improve the supply of new housing to reduce the shortage of residential property was cut short by its defeat in the 1997 general election (Rydin, 2003 p. 49). The incoming New Labour government had already made it clear that there would be no return to the construction of high quantities of publicly owned council housing and thus the valuation of the Labour residential property market was not affected by the change in government (Moran, 2005 p.28).

The New Labour government hoped to control the overvaluing as a by-product of its plans to reduce the national shortage of residential property by building a greater volume of affordable housing which would slow down rising house prices and rents. The targets for affordable housing were arguably not actually high enough to reduce the overvalued price levels within the London residential property market. The New Labour government targets had little discernible impact upon the London residential property market as supply of housing was still outstripped by demand for property within the London area. The inability to have an impact upon the level of affordable housing in London, led to the government giving the Greater London Authority control of achieving central government targets (Mayor of London, September 2007, p. 2). The prices for residential property and rent levels were not lowered due to the time needed for affordable housing projects to fully completed. It can take a few years for new housing projects to be planned, built and completed; time in which the London residential property market could get even further overvalued. The increasingly high values linked with the London residential property market were greatly assisted by the strong economic growth, experienced in the United Kingdom in the early years of the New Labour government, higher growth, falling unemployment and most unusually low inflation as well (UK Residential Property Review, January 2006). High growth and low inflation meant that the Bank of England was able to reduce the interest rates to the lowest levels witnessed in decades. The lowest cost of borrowing in living memory led to people assuming that the cost of mortgages would remain relatively low over a sustained long-term period of time. It also meant that people were more prepared to pay overvalued prices for houses inside the area covered by the London residential property market. However, the period of low interest rates has now come to an end, with several rises being imposed by the Bank of England in order to prevent inflation going above the target levels it is supposed to maintain (UK Residential Property Review, January 2006). PEST analysis could certainly have been used by businesses and organisations in the last few years to predict that the extraordinarily low levels of borrowing could not be sustained indefinitely (.

The demand for housing in the London residential property market has increased during New Labour's time in office because of unprecedented levels of immigration in to Britain. New Labour had relaxed entry regulations for workers from other European Union member states, with millions of Eastern

Europe entering Britain to work. Migrant workers have been attracted to the London area and the South East of England, as that is where work is easiest to find. The other source of immigrants who are increasing the demand for housing within the London residential property market is asylum seekers (Moran, 2005 p.29). New Labour eased the restrictions upon asylum seekers entering Britain, which resulted in a vast increase in the number of immigrants who wanted to live in the London area. Asylum seekers in particular have often needed housing to be provided for them, placing a strain upon local authorities which only have a limited amount of residential property available. The New Labour government was certainly caught by surprise with regard to the high level of immigration in to the country especially after the Eastern European countries became European Union member states in 2004. Even if the government has made more level of estimations of immigration levels it would still have taken years to adequately house everybody that entered Britain in general and who moved into the London area in particular (UK Residential Property Review, January 2006).

The expansion of the London population due to the arrival of immigrants into the city has clearly demonstrated the lack of residential properties available for people that want to be housed within the London area. If the central government does not find ways to increase the number of residential properties available to buy and to let then the value of properties within the London residential property market will continue to rise over a long-term period of time. That is despite allowing for economic recessions and higher interest rate levels (Daily Telegraph, 06/10/2007). Should the value of the London residential property market continue to rise then it could have potentially undesirable social as well as economic consequences that would affect the whole country rather than just London itself. The amount of new houses being constructed for the London residential property market was already inadequate prior to the arrival of mainly Eastern European workers from the new European Union member states and also asylum seekers. Due to the scarcity of even the most basic of residential properties the value of housing bought outright or rented out to tenants in the London residential property market has undeniably increased to the point of being overvalued. In the first five moths of 2007 for instance 59% of the buyers of the most upmarket residential properties were very wealthy foreigners. The British buyers of the other 41% sold were only able to afford to purchase their new homes due to substantial work based bonuses. The size of work bonuses means that interest rate rises are ineffective at reducing the value of the most expensive houses yet can make mortgages too expensive for ever greater numbers of ordinary people (The Independent, 08 May 2007).

Not all the immigrants who have settled within the London area have been unskilled or semi-skilled Eastern European workers or asylum seekers on relatively low wages or social security benefits. Wealthy foreigners have pushed up the value of houses and apartments within the most fashionable parts of London, which has driven up the cost of acquiring residential property in such districts. Foreign football players playing for the London based Premier League clubs are for instance in a strong position to buy or rent the most expensive residential property within the London area (The Independent, 08 May 2007). English football players at these clubs will also be able to afford these houses and at least while they are still playing will not be put off by overvalued prices for residential property in the prime locations inside the London area (UK Residential

Property Review, January 2006). Foreign celebrities as well as business people have also bought more expensive houses and apartments either as a second home or because they have decided to live in Britain, with London being their preferred location. People that have bought housing within the London residential property market in recent years have included Madonna and Roman Abramovich. Although not all the foreign residential property buyers are as famous as Madonna, or as wealthy as Roman Abramovich they have contributed to the much higher valuation levels experienced within the London residential property market during the last decade or so (Daily Telegraph, 06/10/2007).

The sheer spending power that some celebrities and business people have available has meant that in some districts of London the prices being fetched for residential property is now averaging over £1 million, and rental levels have grown at a comparably fast rate also. The increases in residential property prices and rental levels have meant that London has become the most expensive city on the earth when it comes down to buying or to letting residential property. People that have the money to buy even the most expensive housing would not necessarily be included in PEST analysis, yet their spending power means that the Bank of England could rise interest rates higher than would be generally expected. It could also increase the gap between the most expensive districts and the rest of London (The Independent, 08 May 2007).

There is a viewpoint that the high prices that occur within the London residential property market are not overvalued at all. Such a viewpoint is generally put forward by people that hold a neo-liberal economic or political perspective. The holders of neo-liberal views or opinions would regard capitalist market places as the best means of determining the price as well as the value of all goods and services bought and sold within them. From the neo-liberal perspective prices and values within markets can fluctuate greatly, variations that are predominantly linked with the levels of supply and demand at any given time. The neo-liberal perspective towards residential property markets was certainly the dominant approach in Britain before the Second World War. Neo-liberal concepts arguably became dominant again as a result of the social, economic and also the housing policies pursued by the Thatcher government during the 1980s (Moran, 2005 p. 28). Neither the Major government not the New Labour government that succeeded it have attempted to restore the previously more prominent position of the public sector within residential property markets (Rydin, 2003 p. 49). The reduction of public sector involvement has meant that more businesses would find PEST highly influential (Daily Telegraph, 06/10/2007).

The New Labour government affordable housing programmes would certainly not replace the two million or so residential property sold under the auspices of the right to buy scheme and would not be able to dramatically affect the costs of values within the London residential property market (Moran, 2005 p. 28). Instead changes in the supply as well as in the demand for housing will be the primary factors in determining the over all value within the London residential property market. In the most expensive districts such as Belgravia and Knightsbridge the value of residential properties can be fifty per cent than in the rest of London, reaching a staggering £3,000 per square foot (The Independent, 08 May 2007). The increases in interest rates only seemed to have brought a temporary halt to rising residential property prices, by the early part of 2007 the growth in London property prices was 15.6% (The Sunday Times, 10 June 2007). Arguably the inability of interest rate rises to slow down the London residential property market will mean that the Bank of England will increase those rates still further leading to higher unemployment and more people losing their homes (Daily Telegraph, 06/10/2007).

Economic cycles of boom and recession alongside the levels of interest rates set by the Bank of England will alter the levels of demand. Whilst the supply of new or renovated residential property will chiefly be decided by private sector property developers and also by estate agents (Rydin, 2003 p. 49). The wages and other income of those that require housing and the amounts of money that banks and building societies are prepared to lend will continue to determine the ability of individuals to buy housing within the London area. The people that cannot burrow enough to buy property have to rent housing instead (UK Residential Property Review, January 2006). Whether or not the houses within the London residential property market are overvalued could depend on the position of individuals, business, and organisations within that particular market. Individuals attempting to buy or to let residential property when it is so highly priced are more likely to believe that the value of such property is overvalued (Bannock, Baxter, & Davis, 2003 p. 323). On the other hand the individuals, businesses and organisations that sell or let out housing are more likely to argue that the values as well as the prices inside the London residential property market are in fact fair and are not markedly overvalued. Some businesses as well as some homebuyers have proved to be less vulnerable to recession and higher interest rates (UK Residential Property Review, January 2006). The way that some businesses pay their senior executives can help to explain why the London market is not so easily depressed in value in comparison to the rest of the country. Work related bonuses within the City of London were estimated to have totalled £9 billion for the year 2006-2007, with two-thirds of that amount being spent upon the London residential property market (Daily Telegraph, 06/10/2007).

Conclusions

Therefore it can be concluded that the London residential property market wass to a large extent overvalued in terms of the high costs of buying or renting housing in the early 2000s. The value of residential property as with any other good, commodity or service can be calculated in various ways, such as the cost of land, the cost of construction, the cost of reconstruction, as well as the location of the housing. The value of residential property in particular markets or geographical areas can vary within those specific confines or indeed over different periods of time. Residential property will obviously differ in value in comparison with each other due to the size of each building or the different facilities available. For instance, a four bedroom residential property should in theory at least hold a higher value than a two-bedroom house. The more facilities, rooms or land that a residential property includes then the higher the value of the building should be. Accessing the value of housing uses a great deal of logic. However markets do not always act or react in a logical way, hence the usefulness of the PEST business modal in determining whether any specific market is overvalued or not.

Property developers and estate agents have a tendency to value residential property at the same rate as the same or similar buildings the surrounding area. Property developers, estate agents, and individual residential property owners logically find it in their best interests to sell or to let their residential property for the highest possible prices. The PEST business modal does improve the ability of people to understand the market, yet it cannot control the factors it helps to evaluate. On the other hand the people that need to buy or to let residential property are seeking the lowest prices available as well as much value for money as possible. The London residential property market operates within the same theoretical framework as any other market. Buyers have a valuation for the goods they want to buy, whilst sellers generally have a higher valuation for the goods which they supply to the highest bidder.

The main theories that can be related to the London residential property market are those of demand and supply. When supply and demand levels equalise each other out then the value and also the price of goods should be at a realistic level. When supply outstrips the demand for goods then the value and price for those goods will be lower than their nominal worth. Conversely when demand outstrips supply then the value as well as the price of goods will tend to become overvalued.

The buildings contained within the London residential

property market have always tended to have a higher price and therefore value than similar residential property in the rest of Britain. The higher prices and values for the residential property inside the London area are strongly liked with the prominent social, economic and political position of the city within the United Kingdom. More people have needed to work inside the London area and have had the need to buy, rent, or to sell residential property in the London market. London's actual location adds extra value, as well as higher prices to the residential inside its area and that is before the size, facilities, construction and renovation costs of these buildings is actually taken into account. People that work in London generally earn higher salaries than people who work in the rest of the country, yet have to spend more money on buying or renting the residential property that they actually live in do. High prices and high levels of demand do not automatically lead to residential property in specific markets becoming overvalued. The overvaluation of housing within the confines of the London residential property market is related to the supply of buildings to buy or to let inside that area. The greater the scarcity of the supply of residential property then the stronger the position of sellers in the London residential property market becomes. Any PEST analysis will show the propensity of the London market to generate high prices.

Although there has often been a shortfall in the supply of housing within the London residential property market that scarcity has increased markedly since the 1980s in particular. Housing shortages in the London residential property market were considerably eased by the building of council house estates in the London area, the building of new towns to move people away from Greater London, and high rise tower blocks. The public sector thus expanded its position inside the London residential property market, which prevented council houses from becoming overvalued or unaffordable even when the prices and values in the private housing sector were much higher, and in some places were nearly or were actually overvalued. In the privately owned sections of the London residential property market the London residential property market the value of residential properties within it would vary to a large extent according to the growth or the contractions experienced in the British economy taken as a whole.

When the British economy was booming then the value of the residential properties within the London residential property market would increase, whilst during recessions residential property values would decline, and sometimes would decline sharply enough to produce negative equity. However the

London residential property market usually experienced higher rises in value and lower declines in value than the rest of the country, making the London residential property market more susceptible to becoming overvalued. Buying residential property could either be a very sound financial investment or on the other hand it could be an extremely expensive mistake, depending on whether the London residential property market was growing or declining at any given time. By and large it was and still remains the most popular districts that had a tendency to become overvalued within the London area. Residential property in the less fashionable parts of the city had a much lower tendency to become overvalued yet can still become so during periods of strong demand for domestic housing. The use of the PEST business modal as well as supply and demand theories would allow property to be brought and sold at the most opportune moments. Sound judgement and occasionally good luck could be just as useful as theoretical considerations for investors, buyers, sellers, and tenants within the London area.

The balance as well as the value of housing within the London residential property market was fundamentally altered by the economic and housing policies of the Thatcher government which continue to have a strong effect in the present. It was the Thatcher government's popular expansion of the right to buy scheme that made council houses increasingly available for purchase at substantial discounts for council house tenants. The sell off of council houses stimulated the London residential property market as it did the housing markets in the rest of the country, increasing prices and also raising the value of residential properties. In the short-term the sell off of council houses meant that the supply of available residential properties was increased, yet the effective end of new council house construction meant that the supply of housing would decline over the long-term. Housing values and prices in the area of the London residential property market were also at this point in time were also increased by the greater amounts of lending by the high street banks and building societies. Greater amounts of lending which allowed more people to take out the mortgages that they required to buy overvalued and overpriced residential properties.

The consequences of the popularity and the high take up rate of the right to buy scheme were that the London residential property market operated with practically no intervention from the central government and the rapidly declining influence of the local authorities within the London area. The London residential property market thus became increasingly exposed to the fluctuations of market forces. The 1980s were over all a period of boom in the London residential property market whilst the rest of the British economy recovered more slowly from the hard hitting recession that caused record levels of unemployment and industrial decline. The increasing of interest rates and the subsequent recession of the early 1990s slowed the housing boom within the London residential property market down. The increased level of homeownership brought about by the right to buy scheme meant that the recession of the early 1990s had a greater impact upon the London residential property market than the previous recession had done. Perhaps the most noticeable impact of the recession of the early 1990s was that it brought declining values that led to negative equity in the case of some of the previously most overvalued residential properties. Such variations within the market could be predicted by supply and demand theories as well as by using the PEST business modal to evaluate the market. The London market has sometimes being less predictable than markets in other areas, for instance recessions taking longer to reduce the overvaluation of property. It seems certain that housing will continue to be overvalued in the long-term.

Bibliography

Bannock, Baxter, & Davis, (2003) the Penguin Dictionary of Economics, 7th edition, Penguin, London

Daily Telegraph - London property market: London eyes, Prime properties are still selling fast, but super-rich buyers are watching carefully to see how the financial markets recover by Lulu Egerton, online edition 06/10/2007

Fisher J, Denver D, & Benyon J, (2003) Central Debates in British Politics, Longman, London

Grant Stanley, UK Residential Property Review - Report from Grant Stanley, Chartered Surveyors, JANUARY 2006

Greed C, (1996) Investigating Town Planning, Longman, London

Hodgkinson L (2007) the complete guide to investing in property 2nd edition, Kogan Page, London

Jones M and Lowe R (2002) From Beveridge to Blair – The first fifty years of Britain's Welfare State 1948-98, Manchester University Press Manchester and New York

Mayor of London, The Draft Mayor's Housing Strategy -

Consulting on London's housing, September 2007, Greater London Authority

Moran M, (2005) Politic and Governance in the UK, Palgrave, Basingstoke

Rydin Y, (2003) Urban and Environmental Planning in the UK, Palgrave, Basingstoke

Seeley I H, (1996) Building Economics 4th edition, MacMillan Press Limited, Basingstoke

Southall A, (2000) The City – In Time and Space, Cambridge University Press, Cambridge

The Independent - London residential property is the most expensive in the world By Jane Padgham, Published: 08 May 2007

The Sunday Times, June 10, 2007 - The London property market, Peter Conradi, with additional reporting from Lucy Denyer, Jon Neale, Graham Norwood and Tim Dawson

Www.ProvenModels.com

www.ingramcontent.com/pod-product-compliance
Lightning Source LLC
Chambersburg PA
CBHW062115220526
45471CB00010B/3748